T0024023

THE LITTLE BOOK OF
WITCHCRAFT

JUDITH HURRELL

summersdale

THE LITTLE BOOK OF WITCHCRAFT

An Hachette UK Company
www.hachette.co.uk

Summersdale Publishers Ltd
Part of Octopus Publishing Group Limited
Carmelite House
50 Victoria Embankment
LONDON
EC4Y 0DZ
UK

www.summersdale.com

Printed and bound in China

ISBN: 978-1-80007-407-1

Substantial discounts on bulk quantities of Summersdale books are available to corporations, professional associations and other organizations. For details contact general enquiries: telephone: +44 (0) 1243 771107 or email: enquiries@summersdale.com.

The author and the publisher cannot accept responsibility for any misuse or misunderstanding of any information contained herein, or any loss, damage or injury, be it health or otherwise, suffered by any individual or group acting upon or relying on information contained herein.

CONTENTS

) INTRODUCTION (

Life is full of magical moments. Have you ever brewed a steaming cup of herbal tea and marvelled at its incredible powers to soothe and relax you? Maybe you've felt drawn to pebbles on the beach and taken them home to arrange on your mantelpiece. Or perhaps you like to elevate parts of your daily routine with special rituals – think candles by the bath or saying grace before meals. Believe it or not, these everyday acts contain elements of magic and white witchcraft!

The term witchcraft comes from the Old English *wiccecraeft*, which combines *wicca* (masculine) or *wicce* (feminine) – meaning someone who practises sorcery, i.e. a witch – and *craeft* meaning "craft" or "skill". The word often conjures images of black-cloaked crones chanting around a cauldron, but the history of witchcraft is far richer and more colourful.

People from all cultures and backgrounds have been channelling the power of nature, intention and rituals for generations. The practice blends concepts found in magic, sorcery, religion, folklore, theology and diabolism. In some societies, tradition dictates that witches have innate supernatural powers. However, in

Western practice, witchcraft is accessible to ordinary people. Indeed, while witchcraft has often been considered a woman's domain, people of all genders – including non-binary and gender-fluid individuals – are encouraged to explore and identify with the practice.

This beginner's guide will help witches take their first steps into the craft: from channelling the power of crystals and herbs, casting spells and creating personal rituals to finding a coven or developing a solitary practice. So read on to discover the enchanting world of white witchcraft and look forward to tapping into the magical energy at your fingertips!

WHAT IS WHITE WITCHCRAFT?

Traditionally, white magick is the name given to supernatural powers used with the intention to benefit others. Throughout history, white-magick practitioners have been helpers and healers, but they were often marginalized for their efforts and used as scapegoats for society's ills. Some of those accused in the witchcraft trials had been found to be involved in early nursing and midwifery practices.

These days, the divide between white and black magic is slowly disappearing as witches realize that magick isn't binary. After all, most spells aren't intentionally bad or good, black or white. Instead, they're just one person's request to see their truth materialize over others.

That said, this book uses "white magic" to describe magick intended to harness positive forces for self-fulfilment. Think holistic practices that raise and direct energy and nourish and build trust in the wisdom within.

Perhaps that's why white witchcraft is going mainstream. Because what's not to love about knowing your power and putting it into action?

☽ SPELLS TO HELP OTHERS ☾

Time to put down your wand. No matter how much you want to help, casting spells on others without their permission has become taboo. Society has evolved and witches are realizing that interfering with someone else's free will goes against the core value of witchcraft: self-empowerment.

That said, the urge to help is natural and woven into the history of witchcraft. Although the vast majority of scholarship centres on black witchcraft – perhaps due to the horrifying testimonials from the witchcraft trials of the early modern period – there's a long history of white witches and cunning folk doing good work, as acknowledged by Bishop Latimer in 1552, who commented: "A great many of us, when we be in trouble, or lose anything, we run hither and thither to witches or sorcerers, whom we call wise men... seeking aid and comfort at their hands."

These cunning people provided practical remedies for specific problems – including locating lost people and animals, healing and identifying and opposing black witchcraft.

WITCHCRAFT TO HELP THE ENVIRONMENT

Over 40 years ago, an American witch called Starhawk wrote *The Spiral Dance*, a how-to manual on "earth-based spirituality and ecofeminism". This best-selling book is now a mainstay of modern witchcraft. The text serves as a blueprint – or, rather, green-print – for today's eco-conscious witches, who are increasingly involved in climate activism.

Witchcraft and conservation are naturally intertwined: witchcraft encourages a deep relationship with the planet. It invites us to become more attuned and compassionate toward the land. With witchcraft's tradition of service and direct action, eco-activism is a natural next step.

Many witches use witchcraft to add some "oomph" to their activism. Group spells to pray for the environment, placards charged with sigils, charms designed for change and pocket-sized crystals to keep witches grounded, safe and energetic on marches are all helpful.

If that feels like a big step, lighting a candle, meditating and sending energy from afar is just as effective.

WITCHCRAFT FOR A MORE INCLUSIVE SOCIETY

Witchcraft and otherness go hand in hand; so if you're part of a minority group, such as the LGBTQ+ community, you'll be in good company among witches.

Witches were traditionally victimized for challenging societal norms. Fear of sexuality fuelled this suspicion. "When a woman thinks alone she thinks evil," reads the *Malleus Maleficarum*. Witchcraft was a way of taking back stolen power.

The same applies in modern life. In the late nineties, *Buffy the Vampire Slayer* creator Joss Whedon used witchcraft to express queerness. Since the network wouldn't allow Willow and Tara to be intimate, he used magic as a metaphor for sexuality, creating a positive, progressive space for the LGBTQ+ community at the time.

Even on a practical level, witchcraft is inclusive. As a broad category of practices, rather than a single religion, there's room for diversity. The rituals, affirmations and community are uniquely qualified to validate and celebrate all ways of being. The transformation born of this sense of inclusion has the power to be felt throughout society.

WHY PRACTISE WITCHCRAFT?

No matter where you are on your magical journey, heeding the call to practise the craft can be life-changing. If any of the following signs ring true, chances are, witchcraft is for you!

1   You have a spiritual yearning but haven't found a home in formal religion.
2   You're proud to be different or would like to be more comfortable in your own skin.
3   You have a spiritual connection with nature and want to deepen that bond.
4   You're awake to your intuition, or would like to be.
5   You don't believe in coincidences and see signs everywhere.
6   You're superstitious and fascinated by folklore.
7   You enjoy handicrafts and believe they're therapeutic.
8   You're an "old soul", and people often ask you for advice.
9   You feel connected to various deities, or would like to.
10   You would like to bring more ceremony into your life.

) WITCHCRAFT FOR WELLNESS (

Our lives have been in flux over the past few years. The challenges of things such as climate change, political upheaval and the pandemic have led many to reflect on their priorities.

Perhaps it's not surprising then that self-care no longer seems like a luxury – it's become a necessity. While spa visits, socializing and gym memberships are great ways to invest in self-care, they do cost money, and, with people's budgets increasingly stretched, it's just as effective to indulge in simple pleasures: connecting with nature, following the seasons and applying self-help.

Witchcraft is a natural next step for those drawn to gardening, nature, mindfulness, positive thinking and meditation. The rituals of the craft bring a sense of meaning, tradition and magic to self-care, while encouraging reflection and self-empowerment. Meanwhile, connecting with the natural world is grounding and brings a sense of perspective.

Ultimately, witchcraft reminds us we're all part of something larger than ourselves. It's self-help, with soul.

WHAT MAKES A WITCH?

There's no such thing as a wannabe witch. Know that if you're drawn to witchcraft, you already possess the inner magic needed to practise; it's just a case of embracing that power and learning how to use it.

Tuning into your instincts is vital in discovering what kind of witch you might be. Try pinpointing what attracts you to the craft. Some come via nature, their ancestors, culture or passions, while others have an unexplained curiosity.

There are many types of witches practising many variations of the craft and we'll look at some of them here. Perhaps you're fascinated by herbal medicine, like a Kitchen Witch? Maybe you're enchanted by Celtic knots, like a Celtic Witch? Have you ever turned to the sky for answers, like a Cosmic Witch? These yearnings are signs, lighting the paths before you.

Still not feeling it? No matter how quiet the call, know it's there. You don't need a label. Your witchcraft is yours alone, so enjoy being a free spirit!

SOLITARY WITCH

A Solitary Witch practises alone, outside of a coven – either through choice or because they've yet to find their tribe. Legend has it that Solitary Witches are the reincarnations of witches from generations past. Their innate abilities and intuitive knowing often awaken at puberty, so they have less need for a coven than witches without an ancestry in the craft.

HEDGE WITCH

This title pays homage to the wise women of old who lived their lives beyond the boundaries of the village. They also practise alone. The word "hedge" is a nod to the boundary between this world and the spirit realm – the veil between these worlds is very thin for Hedge Witches.

As the name implies, Hedge Witches feel a calling from the natural world, often taking inspiration from the magical properties of their land. Hedge Witches typically see magic all around them and let it infuse their day-to-day activities.

KITCHEN WITCH

The Kitchen Witch elevates the everyday activity of cooking to a magical level. Their kitchen apothecary is stocked with fresh, local herbs, aromatic spices and forgotten ingredients of old. By preparing most of their meals from scratch and tailoring them to suit their intention, the Kitchen Witch turns every meal into medicine. However, this isn't just about ingredients. The Kitchen Witch also has magical powers of their own, which they infuse into their cooking. Within their homes you may also find kitchen altars housing sacred seasonal ingredients.

GREEN WITCH

The Green Witch lives in deep connection with the land. They feel most alive when working on their garden, spending time in green spaces or celebrating Mother Nature. Green Witches are often inspired by the plants, trees and wildlife around them, perhaps casting spells using local ingredients or divining the future from natural signs. They're always sure to tread lightly and never exploit nature's bounty.

SEA WITCH

The Sea Witch enjoys a deep intimacy with the sea. You'll find them combing the seashore for magical tools, swimming in nature or being lulled to sleep by the waves. They have a deep respect for all water and harness its properties when casting spells to heal, protect, cleanse and draw abundance.

ELEMENTAL WITCH

Elemental Witches call on the powers of earth, air, wind, water and fire when casting spells or performing rituals. They may have altars devoted to the elements or feel drawn to one aspect in particular.

COSMIC WITCH

Cosmic Witches look to the cosmos, astrology and astronomy to bring celestial energy to their practice. These witches become familiar with the solar system, basing their spells and rituals on the changing patterns.

HEREDITARY WITCH

These witches pass witchcraft to their family members, from mother to daughter or father to son, but rarely outside the bloodline. This isn't about innate genetic ability. Instead, Hereditary Witches pass on learned knowledge and traditions, which are often kept secret from outsiders.

SECULAR WITCH

While Secular Witches cast spells and use crystals, herbs and candles, they don't believe their powers are spiritual. They are non-religious and don't worship higher beings. Deities aren't a complete no-no, however. A Secular Witch can still believe in a higher power; they just don't connect this to their craft.

HEARTH WITCH

Hearth Witches are homebodies who like nothing more than to hunker down amid familiar comforts. Perhaps through candle-making, handicrafts, cookery or tending houseplants, they focus their energies on creating a sacred space at home.

TRADITIONAL WITCH

The Traditional Witch takes their lead from an old craft that existed before Wicca emerged in the 1950s. They often commune with the spirits of their ancestors, honour the history of their land and study folklore passed down through generations.

GARDNERIAN AND ALEXANDRIAN WICCANS

Wicca is a traditional form of modern witchcraft that surfaced soon after the repeal of the Witchcraft Act in 1951 in Great Britain. Gardnerian Wiccans can trace their unbroken lineage back to its founder, Gerald Gardner. Wicca is a formalized belief system with oath-bound traditions and initiations, meaning those initiated must keep their knowledge secret.

Alexandrian Wiccans can trace their lineage back to Alex Sanders, one of Gardner's earliest initiates. Founded in the 1960s, Alexandrian Wicca is an eclectic version of Gardnerian Wicca, combining ceremonial magic with the Kabbalah (an ancient Jewish mystical tradition).

MYTH-BUSTING

Green-tinged skin, pointy hats, broomsticks – if you've been on the lookout for a conventional witch, chances are you haven't found one yet.

Witches are a misunderstood bunch, plagued by stereotypes. At worst, witchcraft is branded evil, Satan worship. At best, witches are figures of Halloween fun.

Even positive representations can miss the point. In mainstream media, witches are often feminist figures, using witchcraft to take on the patriarchy. Think *Buffy the Vampire Slayer*'s Willow Rosenberg (Alyson Hannigan) and Disney's Maleficent (Angelina Jolie). "We are the granddaughters of the witches you weren't able to burn" – paraphrased from Tish Thawer's novel *The Witches of BlackBrook* is a popular slogan in feminist protest. But even this stereotype oversimplifies things.

Yes, witchcraft is inherently feminist, but that's because it's about self-determination – for everyone, regardless of sex, gender, sexual orientation, ethnicity, disability or age. Witchcraft is about owning your power, harnessing natural energy and becoming the best version of yourself.

Let's take a minute to dispel some common myths about witchcraft.

"WITCHCRAFT IS EVIL"

Witches don't deserve their bad rep. While hexes and black magick exist in some branches of the craft, witches are no more likely to be wicked than the next person.

Many witches follow a version of the "Threefold Law" from the Wiccan Rede – the moral code of Wicca – which states that anything a person wishes upon others returns to them three times over.

This code also affirms, "an it harm none, do what ye will." In modern English, this translates as, "if it harms none, do what you will," emphasizing Wiccans' personal responsibility to prevent harm to others.

"WITCHES FOLLOW SATAN"

This myth makes no sense. Most witches don't even believe in the devil, let alone worship him. The devil and hell are early Judaeo-Christian concepts, with no place in Wiccan or other witchcraft traditions.

That said, Wiccans don't believe in one almighty god either. Instead, Wiccans believe in many gods and goddesses, much like Buddhists and Hindus do. Other witches are not religious at all.

"ALL WITCHES ARE FEMALE"

Witchcraft isn't an exclusive clique only open to cis, white, straight, non-disabled women. Yes, women have a rich history in witchcraft, partly because it's empowered them in a male-dominated system – but witchcraft is inclusive: anyone practising witchcraft can call themselves a witch.

Historically speaking, it's worth remembering that although generally more women were prosecuted for witchcraft during the Burning Times, many thousands of men were also tried and executed. Even now, people worldwide – including children – are still persecuted and killed over accusations of witchcraft.

"WITCHES ARE BORN INTO WITCHCRAFT"

This is not *Harry Potter*. You don't have to be "pureblood" to be included in witchcraft. Although many witchcraft festivals and rituals include a hat-tip to the ancestors, this doesn't automatically assume a witchy lineage. Likewise, if you'd prefer not to acknowledge your family tree, this has no bearing on your ability to be a witch. Many witches use the word ancestor in the broadest possible sense. Witchcraft is open to everyone.

"WITCHCRAFT IS A RELIGION"

Some witches follow Wicca, worshipping the Triple Goddess (see page 113) and the Horned God (see page 114). Others revere deities found in other cultures, such as the Greek goddess Gaia or the Norse god Thor. Yet more worship nature through ceremonies based on the Wheel of the Year (see page 41). But witchcraft doesn't require any worship at all, which is why witches are such a diverse group.

"WITCHES ARE GRUMPY OLD WOMEN"

This myth might seem harmless, but for some sociologists, the Halloween caricature of a cantankerous old hag is a form of symbolic violence. For example, Dr Maggie Webster, whose PhD thesis looked at witch- and faith-identities within social media, believes this treatment manipulates and controls societies' perception of older women by presenting them as untrustworthy or mad. In other words, imposing the hag-witch stereotype on women is a form of non-physical violence. Time to look beyond the stereotypes!

✦ ✦ A BRIEF HISTORY OF WITCHCRAFT ✦ ✦

Witchcraft has survived a turbulent history to become a mainstream phenomenon today. In pre-Christian Europe, what we now call witchcraft was just a natural way of life. Pagans worshipped nature and multiple deities. Wise healers and seers offered help through herbal medicines, rituals and divination.

However, from the seventh century onward, attitudes darkened. In medieval times, fears over so-called "black magic" meant critics felt all witchcraft was potentially harmful or somehow linked to the devil.

Things worsened in the sixteenth and seventeenth centuries, when an estimated 40,000 to 60,000 people were executed in Europe's witch trials through burning, drowning and hanging. In the US, around 110,000 people were tried for witchcraft and between 40,000 to 60,000 were executed.

Eventually, authority figures in the Age of Enlightenment began to doubt the proceedings, poking holes in the trials. When the UK's "Witchcraft Laws" were repealed in 1951, multiple traditions began to spring up.

Today, those practising witchcraft number in the millions, with more coming out of the "broom closet" every day.

❯ CULTURAL NOTE ❮

This brief history focuses on the twists and turns of witchcraft in the West. It sheds light on its humble pagan beginnings, the gruesome witch trials of the sixteenth and seventeenth centuries and the birth of modern witchcraft in the 1950s.

However, this history is just one aspect of the story. Unfortunately, throughout history, Western Christian colonizers have used the word "witchcraft" to demonize the spiritual practices of indigenous peoples, justifying their oppression. Indeed, the English label "witchcraft" oversimplifies many beliefs and traditions that still thrive worldwide. Followers past and present don't always identify with the word.

Therefore, it's essential to recognize the difference between folk magic and formal religions born from slavery, such as the African-based religions of Santería, Voodoo and Candomblé. It's also important to remember that there are still regions in which people are persecuted and even killed in organized witch hunts, especially in Africa, Southeast Asia, Saudi Arabia and Latin America.

) ANCIENT BEGINNINGS (

Magic and witchcraft have a story as old as time. Here are just some examples of how witchcraft has been used throughout the centuries:

- Witchcraft of some sort has existed since humans gathered in groups. Almost all traditional societies used offerings, charms and simple rituals.

- Early Shamans used magical tools and rituals to contact the dead in probably the earliest form of religion: Shamanism.

- In 4500–c.1900 BCE, ancient Sumerian and Babylonian witches fought demons using magical amulets, incantations and exorcisms.

- The ancient Egyptians attempted to manipulate the gods in their favour using amulets, spells and magical formulas.

- In 800 BCE, the ancient Greeks hailed Hecate the "Queen of Witchcraft".

- In Homer's *Odyssey*, Circe – the first witch in Western literature – turned men into animals.

- The Greeks practised Theurgy: a magical religion that used rituals to evoke action from the gods.

- From 700 BCE to 100 CE the Celts thrived in northern Europe. Their pagan beliefs, reverence of nature and seasonal rituals inspired many practices that were later labelled witchcraft.

- Around 560 BCE, Exodus and Leviticus, two Old Testament books, denounced witches in an attempt to persuade Jews to stick to their religious practices rather than those of local tribes.

- Around 0 CE, the Celts revered the "Witch Goddess" Calleach in the Samhain festival, the precursor to Halloween.

- Circa 420 CE, St Augustine of Hippo dismissed pagan magic and religion as a lure of the devil.

- In the ninth century, the Church influenced civil law to create anti-witchcraft rules with a sly linguistic tweak. They extended the Latin term for harmful magic, maleficium, to cover all forms of magic.

- Meanwhile in legends, witchcraft flourished: the shape-shifting enchantress and healer of Arthurian legend, Morgan le Fay, ruled Avalon in Geoffrey of Monmouth's *Vita Merlini* (c.1150) while the medieval Welsh goddess Ceridwen was said to have made potions in her cauldron.

☽ THE WITCH TRIALS ☾

In the mid-1400s, witchcraft trials erupted in Europe. St Joan of Arc (1412–1431) was just one of thousands burned at the stake for heretic beliefs, including witchcraft.

In 1486, German witch-finder Heinrich Kramer wrote *Malleus Maleficarum* (Hammer of the Witches), outselling every publication in Europe except the Bible. The terrifying book featured women having sex with random passing demons, killing babies and even stealing penises.

The Reformation soon followed, dividing Europe between Protestants and those loyal to the Pope. The upheaval sent kill-rates rocketing, with leaders on both sides keen to prove their godliness. Germany, already rife with sectarian strife, saw Europe's highest execution rate.

In 1571, the court of Charles IX accused Trois Echelles, a dreaded French sorcerer, of witchcraft. He claimed thousands of fellow witches roamed France, causing witch hysteria to spread like wildfire. Then, when James VI and I married Anne of Denmark in 1589, he became fascinated with Denmark's history of witch persecution and brought the phenomenon to the British Isles.

One of King James' first victims was Agnes Sampson in 1591. Her tortured confession claimed 200 witches had sailed in sieves to North Berwick at Halloween to take down the king.

The resulting witch-hunt – the largest in British history – condemned dozens of witches to death. It's rumoured that "Bald Agnes" haunts Holyrood Palace and inspired Shakespeare's sisters in *Macbeth*.

Between 1591 and 1662, further waves of panic erupted, making Scotland's death toll particularly high.

James identified ways to uncover witches in his book *Daemonologie*, including the "witches mark" – a spot on the body that felt no pain.

The Burning Times spread to England, with the famous Pendle witch trial occurring in 1612. The testimony of a nine-year-old girl led to the execution of nine people.

In 1682, Temperance Lloyd, a senile woman from Bideford, became the last witch to be executed in England. At the time, Lord Chief Justice Sir Francis North branded the prosecution profoundly flawed.

) THE PENDLE WITCH TRIALS (

The Pendle witch trials are one of the most notorious witch trials of the seventeenth century. Ten people were convicted of witchcraft and went to the gallows on the moors above Lancaster.

The trial was unusual because Thomas Potts, the court's clerk, documented it in *The Wonderfull Discoverie of Witches in the Countie of Lancaster*, fuelling the legend.

Six of the witches on trial were from rival families, the Demdikes and Chattoxs, led by the old widows Elizabeth Southerns ("Old Demdike") and Anne Whittle ("Mother Chattox"). Old Demdike had been practising magic and trading herbs and medicines in the village for 50 years. But suspicion from King James I meant the climate was changing and people were becoming uneasy about witchcraft.

It all started with Alizon Device – a granddaughter of Old Demdike – and a pedlar, John Law. On the road to Trawden Forest, Alizon asked John for some pins – it's not clear whether she was buying or begging. When John refused, Alizon cursed him. Soon after, John suffered a stroke, which he blamed on Alizon.

Alizon admitted telling the devil to lame John before Justice Nowell. Then, motivated by a long-term feud, accused the Chattox family of bewitching and killing four people. The family retaliated, pointing the finger at Old Demdike, accusing her of witchcraft.

At court, family members turned on each other and pointed fingers, leading to confessions from both sides. The judge detained Alizon, Old Demdike, Old Chattox and Chattox's daughter and planned a trial.

The story should have ended there, but Alizon's brother stole a neighbour's sheep at a meeting for family supporters. As a result, the judge felt compelled to summon a further eight people for questioning and trial. Old Demdike died in the dungeon before reaching trial. Of the 11 who went to trial in August 1612, 10 were found guilty and executed by hanging. Alizon's younger sister, Jennet Device, was a key witness, giving fatal evidence against her own family at just nine years old.

Some Pendle witches seemed convinced they were guilty, including Alizon Device, who fell to her knees in a teary confession before John Law in court.

❯ THE SALEM WITCH TRIALS ❮

Between February 1692 and May 1693, a series of witchcraft trials took place in colonial Massachusetts, leading to 20 executions – including 14 women. Five others, including two children, died in prison. The trials followed 12 previous executions for witchcraft in the area during the seventeenth century.

Like their European counterparts, the Puritans of New England lived in fear of a judgemental God, the devil and his handmaidens – otherwise known as witches. Society viewed women as more vulnerable to the devil, so they were susceptible to witchcraft allegations. Women healers with knowledge of anything deemed "pagan" were particularly at risk.

In February 1692, two young girls in Salem village – Abigail Williams and Betty Parris – started having bizarre fits after experimenting with fortune-telling techniques. A doctor found no signs of illness. The hysteria spread and other young women started fitting, too. Witchcraft accusations began to surface.

The bewitched girls pointed fingers at three outsiders; Sarah Good (a homeless beggar), Sarah Osborne (an infrequent church-goer) and Tituba (an enslaved person). The outcasts were arrested and left to defend themselves.

As more young girls came out as victims of witchcraft, a wave of allegations led to 200 accusations – including citizens in good standing and at least one child. Colonists began to fear anyone could be a witch.

Of the 200 people accused, 30 were found guilty. The Puritan authorities hanged 19 people on Gallows Hill. A 71-year-old man was pressed to death for refusing to plead and at least five people died in jail.

The trials were one of the most notorious episodes of mass hysteria in colonial America: a cautionary tale against paranoia, isolationism, religious extremism, false accusations and lapses of due process.

THE BIRTH OF
MODERN WITCHCRAFT

In 1951, British laws prohibiting witchcraft were repealed, bringing witchcraft into the open. In 1954, Gerald Gardner – a practising witch – published *Witchcraft Today* and went on to establish Wicca.

Gardner first heard the word wicca – which means "wise people" in Scots English – when he was initiated into a coven in the 1930s. His book described oath-bound, initiatory and secret traditions based on ancient Eastern mysticism, Kabbalah and British legend.

Splinter groups soon formed, establishing new traditions. But most Wiccan groups share similar principles:

- They see nature as divine.

- They worship gods and goddesses.

- They believe in karma, an afterlife and honouring ancestry.

- They mark seasonal changes.

- Their motto is "harm none".

- They respect other belief systems.

- They use magic and spell-work to harness natural energy and effect change.

CONTEMPORARY WITCHCRAFT

In the 1960s and 70s, Wicca spread from the UK to other English-speaking countries. Flourishing feminist and environmental movements adopted it and the religion evolved.

In Britain, several strands developed. Gardnerians trace their lineage back to Gerald Gardner, who revived the modern craft. Alexandrians are descendants of Alex and Maxine Sanders, who developed Gardner's ideas. Witches with practices that pre-date Wicca call themselves Traditionalists, while Hereditaries can trace their tradition through generations of their family. Feminist principles characterize the Dianic Craft, while Hedge Witches follow a more solitary path.

However, these schools of thought are just part of the story. Many witches don't identify as Wiccan. Some call themselves Pagan, Druid or nothing at all. Indeed, when it comes to witchcraft, spiritual boundaries are blurred and entirely optional. As a result, secular witchcraft, with no spiritual leaning, is also thriving. All labels aside: the #WitchTok hashtag currently clocks up over 20.7 billion views on TikTok!

PRACTISING WITCHCRAFT

Getting started with witchcraft can create an urge to splurge! Social media channels featuring gothic cauldrons, glittering chunks of crystal and altars chock-full of beautiful witchy props can be inspiring, but throwing money at your new hobby is entirely optional.

Self-empowerment is at the heart of witchcraft. You are enough, just as you are. While props, tools or trinkets can help evoke the witchy vibe, you're powerful all on your own.

Likewise, harnessing the power of resources at your fingertips is the essence of witchcraft. The practice was born in the natural world, using the tools witches found around them. So channelling sentimental or foraged

treasures will always be meaningful. If you're the crafty type, why not make your own? It's a good idea to build your collection slowly; props and tools become more potent as you develop relationships with them.

☽ BROOMSTICK ☾

Don't be put off by domestic drudgery; the broomstick has an illicit history! Some experts believe witches of old greased their broom handles with mind-altering herbs. So rather than ingesting hallucinogenic substances, witches could absorb them through their skin – by riding their brooms. Instead of flying, perhaps witches were getting high? Witches also used broomsticks – sometimes called besoms – to sweep away dirt and negative energy.

While we advise against using brooms for hallucinogenic purposes, they're still suitable for cleansing rituals. Making your own is simple.

Traditionally, witches fashioned bristles from bundles of birch twigs. Birch trees sprout leaves early so they're linked with new beginnings. Naturally antiseptic, birch is also associated with purification. Broom handles were traditionally fashioned from oak – for strength, or ash – for prophecy. Willow wands bound the broom together in a hat-tip to Hecate, goddess of witchcraft. These days, any wood, herbs or plants are suitable.

☽ WAND ☾

Clichéd maybe, but the wand is a popular tool in witchcraft due to its rich symbolism and magical purposes.

Witches can use wands for directing energy, consecrating space, invoking deities or simple divination. A phallic symbol, it represents male energy, power and virility. That said, in *The Odyssey* by Homer, the goddess Circe uses her wand to turn men into animals.

Witches traditionally fashioned wands from wood. Fallen tree branches were considered a gift from the tree, with special powers and energies linked to each species. Think blackthorn for protection, apple for eternal youth and fertility, hazel for creativity and love, elder for regeneration and beech for wisdom. However, any wand that feels like it belongs in your hand is suitable. So why not go down to the woods to find your own? Be sure to thank the tree for sharing.

☽ CAULDRON ☾

"Double, double toil and trouble, fire burn and cauldron bubble," say the witches in Shakespeare's *Macbeth*, and there's no denying black, gothic cauldrons are synonymous with the craft.

The cauldron's origins, however, are down to earth: our ancestors used these everyday objects for everything from making soup to laundry in the days of open fires. But that doesn't mean they aren't symbolic. For many witches, the receptacle represents the goddess and her womb. Likewise, cauldrons are transformational places where humble ingredients combine to become greater than the sum of their parts.

Witches still find many practical uses for a cauldron, from making potions and mixing herbs and spices for spells, to burning petitions and holding candles. Some even use them as decorations on their altars. If you don't have a cast-iron pot handy, a bowl, wok, slow cooker, saucepan or even a bathtub will do just as well!

THE MAGICAL YEAR

Witches often look to the seasons to bring rhythm to their practice, marking specific points in the earth's journey around the sun.

Celebrations centre around astronomical events, so the dates vary every year, but there's always something to look forward to with a celebration every six weeks. These include the summer solstice, winter solstice, spring equinox, autumn equinox and the midpoints between them.

Each Pagan tradition has its own name for these days, but, generally, the four solar events are called "quarter days", or fire festivals, and the midpoint events are "cross-quarter days".

Witches call this cycle the Wheel of the Year. Wiccans call the special days "sabbaths", harking back to Gerald Gardner's claim that the name was passed down from the Middle Ages when the name for the Jewish Shabbat intermingled with terms from other religious celebrations to indicate a day of rest.

We usually see time as linear in the modern world, but the Wheel of the Year recognizes the cyclical nature of life, drawing attention to what's gained and lost in each phase.

) WINTER AND EARLY SPRING (

Yule, or the winter solstice, on December 20, 21, 22 or 23 marks the longest night in the northern hemisphere. It's the darkest point when the sun stops its decline. Instead, at Yule, it hovers on the cusp of turning, rising in the same place for a few days. For Wiccans, this is the time when the goddess gives birth to the sun god. Then, as the sun enters this new phase, Wiccans celebrate the return of the light.

The symbol of the evergreen tree reminds witches of nature's resilience in the depth of winter. Burning a yule log symbolizes the rebirth of light. Many witches save a chunk of each year's yule log for next year's fire as a symbol of continuity and survival. So why not decorate a log with seasonal foliage and start the tradition this year?

Imbolc, Brigid or Brigid's Day or Candlemas, on February 1 or 2 in the northern hemisphere or August 1 or 2 in the southern hemisphere, is a time to shake off winter and prepare for a fresh start. A time of fertility, hope and looking to the future, embodied by the Celtic goddess Brigid.

For Wiccans, Imbolc is a time when the earth is awakening and the life force is stirring. Witches often "spring clean" their homes and set intentions for the coming year. Some weave Brigid dolls or crosses from corn, wheat or willow to keep evil and hunger at bay. Others bake seed cakes to celebrate new life.

Recipe for seed cakes

Cream 120 g (4 oz) of butter and 120 g (4 oz) of caster sugar until light and fluffy. Beat in three large eggs. When combined, add ½ tsp caraway seeds, ½ tsp poppy seeds, 170 g (6 oz) self-raising flour, 50 g (2 oz) ground almonds, and 35 ml (2 tbsp) milk, beating well. Pour into a paper-lined loaf tin and bake for an hour at 160°C/320°F/gas mark 3.

) SPRING AND EARLY SUMMER (

Ostara, Eostar or spring equinox is celebrated on March 20, 21, 22 or 23 in the northern hemisphere, or September 22 or 23 in the southern hemisphere. It's a point of balance when day and night are equal in length. But the light soon wins out, and the evenings begin to stretch. The natural world is coming alive.

Originally a celebration of the Germanic goddess Eostre/Ostara and her connections to fertility, renewal and rebirth, the event evolved into Easter when Christianity took hold. Symbols include eggs, which signify new life, and hares – Ostara herself has the head of a hare. Instead of simply decorating eggs this year, why not write your intentions on the shell? Then, on Ostara night, crush the shell and sprinkle it into the soil. Plant a seed underneath it, chanting:

Little charm, made of shell,
I ask the earth to hear my spell.
May all things grow. May all things flow.
Blessing at the turning of the Wheel.

You can then look forward to seeing your intentions grow and come to life during the spring!

Beltane, May Eve or May Day on April 30 or May 1 marks the peak of spring. In the southern hemisphere it's celebrated on November 1. The energies of the earth are at their strongest, turning potential into reality. For Wiccans, it's a time when the goddess (Flora, the Goddess of Spring, the May Queen or the May Bride) and the god (the Green Man, Oak King or Jack-in-the-Green) marry. The ancient fertility festival was a time to light fires, drink mead and make love in the woods!

Traditionally, Beltane kicked off when the hawthorn, or May tree, blossomed. Legend has it that young women bathed in its dew as a beauty aid. So why not go for a walk at sunrise, gather some flowers and anoint yourself?

) SUMMER AND EARLY AUTUMN (

When the sun rises on June 20, 21, 22 or 23, we enjoy the longest day of the year in the northern hemisphere, known as Litha, summer solstice or Midsummer's Day. In the southern hemisphere it is celebrated on December 21 or 22. Today, light triumphs and nature thrives.

For Wiccans, the goddess is now heavily pregnant, and the sun god is strong. Of course, this high point also comes with a whisper of darkness. From today, the sun will begin to wane. But for now, with abundance everywhere, it's time to celebrate! So why not light a Litha bonfire to enjoy the long evening? Don't forget to dress for the occasion with a crown made from seasonal flowers.

For the ancient pagans, emotions ran high at Lammas or Lughnasadh on August 1, when people came together to celebrate the first harvest. In the southern hemisphere this is celebrated on February 1. Feelings of gratitude for the harvest combined with fears of the looming winter. Land disputes also tended to flare up at the Lammas festival. Modern Wiccans use this time to give thanks, face their fears, reassess and build their resilience. It's a good time to bake bread to share with friends. Try singing this blessing while kneading your dough.

With this loaf
I knead and bake
I freely give
and freely take.
Thanks for the harvest
Thanks for the bread
Thanks for the light
In dark days ahead.

❯ AUTUMN AND EARLY WINTER ❮

Mabon, fall equinox or harvest falls on September 20, 21, 22 or 23 in the northern hemisphere, when the day and the night are equal in length. In the southern hemisphere this is celebrated on March 21. Sap is returning to the trees' roots, changing the green of summer into the fire of autumn.

Mabon coincides with the grain harvest. It's time to reap what was sown at Imbolc and give thanks for summer's bounty before winter descends.

For Wiccans, the goddess is radiant as Harvest Queen, and the god is dying with the last of the grain. Witches like to give thanks and reflect on the year's manifestations at this time. So why not start a gratitude journal? Be sure to pick out things that genuinely raise a smile, rather than things you feel you ought to acknowledge. Genuine gratitude creates feel-good vibes and sends a signal to the universe for more, please!

For many witches in the northern hemisphere, October 31 or November 1 hosts the year's main "sabbath"; Samhain, All Hallow's Eve or Hallowmas. The southern hemisphere equivalent falls on April 30 or May 1. Samhain represents death at the end of the cycle. As the world descends into darkness, it's time to remember the ancestors.

Traditionally, the veils between the spirit world and ours are at their thinnest now. So why not create an altar to honour your ancestors, departed loved ones or witches past? Gather pictures or trinkets and arrange them among seasonal treasures. Give thanks for their gifts and the gifts of the season by saying this blessing:

As the wheel turns here on earth
Today I celebrate death and rebirth.
And while the veil is thin and clear
I'll invite my ancestors near.

Ghosts and spirits, hear my prayer
Carried through the autumn air
Like the owl hooting in the moonlit tree
Draw close and speak to me.

And as the sun sinks in the west
Ancestors, watch me as I rest.
Keep me safe and without fear,
On Samhain night, the Witches' New Year.

CRYSTALS AND GEMSTONES

Who doesn't love a bit of bling? Crystals are a beautiful way to witchify your space, but they have a fascinating history too.

Legends of crystal magic date back to the continent of Atlantis, whose people were said to have used crystals for telepathic communication. In the real world, historians have found records of ancient Sumerians – the people of southern Mesopotamia – using crystals in magical formulas as far back as c.4500 BCE. British archaeologists have unearthed a Balkan Bronze Age amber necklace in northwest England, which, they believe, must have been prized due to the distance it travelled. Similarly, they've found Neolithic, Bronze Age and Iron Age graves from c.4000 BCE to 50 CE, containing layers of quartz used to cover, hide or protect the body.

So why did our ancestors value crystals? Writings from 400 BCE reveal that the ancients believed crystal amulets and talismans could offset negative happenings. Read on to learn how to tap into their ancient magical powers.

) CULTURAL NOTE (

Crystal emporiums can feel like spiritual sweet shops, so it's hard to believe the industry can be charged with bad vibes. But crystals are a non-renewable resource, raising issues of sustainability. In addition, miners and production workers are frequently low-paid, underage and work in unsafe conditions. Meanwhile, a lack of regulations enables exploitation. Therefore, it's vital to shop carefully. Good questions to ask suppliers include:

- Do you source your crystals ethically?

- Do you know where they come from and who owns the mines?

- Are the workers treated and paid fairly?

Steer clear of cheap crystals with unknown provenance. Instead, look for suppliers in countries with fair labour standards. Crystals mined in the US and Canada, for example, are ethical by default thanks to strict labour laws. In some parts of the world, it's still possible to explore and dig for buried treasure yourself.

) CRYSTALS TO TREASURE (

AGATE

Focusing – reassuring – revealing

People have been collecting agates since prehistoric times. They can still be found loose on beaches all over the world. Their intricate patterns result from volcanic lava bubbles cooling and filling with crystalline bands.

Witches use agate to enhance perception, analytical abilities and concentration. Agate also instils a sense of security and safety. Be sure only to buy agate from ethical sources such as the US and the UK.

AMBER

Balancing – pain-relieving – protective

Witches believe this fossilized tree resin helps to balance emotions, build resilience and soothe pain. For centuries parents have strung amber necklaces around their babies to ease teething pain and keep them from harm. Geologists aren't sure how long amber takes to form but believe that most specimens are between 30–90 million years old. The oldest amber discovered is 320 million years old. Shoppers should look for amber from ethical sources including the UK, New Zealand and the US.

AMETHYST

Cleansing – calming – clearing

A form of quartz, amethyst ranges from purple to violet in colour. Historically it's been used in healing and rituals connected to the mind, mental health, intuition and clarity: the ancient Greeks carried it to avoid drunkenness! Amethyst also comes into its own when cleansing and consecrating sacred space. If you're shopping for amethyst, look for ethically mined examples from the US and Canada.

CITRINE

Manifesting – empowering – energizing

Many witches believe citrine harnesses the sun's power – it's a life-giving stone that awakens creativity, inspires action and creates success. Nicknamed the merchant's stone, it's useful in spells for manifestation and abundance, helping witches seize the day and live life to the full. Brazil is home to large deposits of citrine, where environmental laws mean the gem-mining industry must adhere to environmental regulations. Other ethical sources include France, Spain and North Carolina in the US.

FLUORITE

Stimulating – unblocking – communicating

Many believe fluorite is an antidote for blockages in the throat chakra – one of many energy points found in the body according to ancient meditation practices. Witches use fluorite to encourage truth-telling and self-expression. Look out for unique examples from the Rogerley Mine in Durham, UK – home to blue-green fluorites that change colour in UV light. Other ethical sources include the US and New Zealand.

HEMATITE

Healing – strengthening – protective

Shiny grey hematite is a highly magnetic natural form of iron that's popular in magical work. When sliced thinly, it reveals a deep red, which led the Vikings to call it the "blood stone", believing it stopped fallen soldiers from bleeding. Hematite was also a common stone in mourning jewellery and is used frequently in feng shui due to its protective qualities. Witches sometimes place stones around their windows and doors to ward off negative energies. Shoppers should look for ethically sourced hematite from the UK, US or Canada.

JET

Protective – purifying – lucky

For centuries, mourners have turned to jet to draw out negativity and usher in positivity. Indeed, it was a favourite of Queen Victoria after the death of her husband, Prince Albert. The Romans believed that jet protected against the "evil eye". Folklore also suggests fans of jet used it as a lucky charm. The finest specimens are found on England's northeast coast, particularly on Whitby beach, but other good sources include France, Spain and the US.

NEPHRITE JADE

Manifesting – pain-relieving – calming

Sometimes called the stone of dreams, nephrite jade is a powerful manifestor, and comes in various colours, including yellow, grey, black and green. It was also used as a pain reliever for centuries: the word jade is a translation of the Spanish phrase "piedra de ijada", which means "stone for pain in the side". Nephrite jade stills the mind and invites clarity and confidence. Look for ethically sourced crystals from Canada and New Zealand.

ROSE QUARTZ

Loving – compassionate – comforting

If you've ever tuned in to the #witchcore hashtag on social media, you'll know rose quartz is a must-have. Witches love it for its heart-opening qualities, with many believing it's the stone of unconditional love. The ancient Romans and Greeks honoured rose quartz, linking it to their goddesses of love: Venus and Aphrodite. Rose quartz is more abundant in South Dakota, US, than anywhere else in the world, so you can shop guilt-free. It's also mined in Australia.

SMOKY QUARTZ

Grounding – manifesting – soothing

Traditionally nicknamed the stone of cooperation, witches use smoky quartz in spells to improve relationships. It also dulls feelings of stress and is sometimes referred to as a spiritual sedative. In addition, its earthy colouring gives it a grounding, anchoring quality. Smoky quartz is also an excellent stone for manifestation, helping dreams become a reality. Look for ethically sourced crystals from the US or Australia.

TURQUOISE

Protective – harmonizing – lucky

One of the oldest known gemstones, beautiful sea-green turquoise represents protection, harmony and good fortune. A famous good luck charm, witches use turquoise in spells to attract success and wealth. The stone is also used in love magic as a token to bring harmony to existing relationships. Unfortunately, some sources say that the stone's colour will fade if love wanes. Look for turquoise from ethical sources such as the US.

WHITE QUARTZ

Magical – healing – insightful

Quartz is one of the earth's most abundant minerals, often nicknamed the "backyard gemstone". Exceptional examples pop up in Northern Ireland, thanks to its complex and varied local geology.

Witches view quartz stones as master healers, believing they facilitate growth and awareness. White quartz brings clarity to the wearer and enhances communication between the higher self and spirit guides. Shop for ethically sourced examples from the US, Australia and the UK.

THE POWER OF HERBS

Herbal medicine is far from a new-age phenomenon: since before records began, people have turned to plants for their healing and magical qualities.

In Lascaux, France, Palaeolithic peoples depicted herbal remedies in cave paintings dating back to 13,000 and 25,000 BCE. Meanwhile, the ancient Egyptians valued myrrh, frankincense, cinnamon and cassia. And explorers in the 1920s even found perfume in Tutankhamen's tomb.

The ancient Greeks and Romans went crazy for herbs and aromatics, with Hippocrates proclaiming, "let thy food be thy medicine and thy medicine be thy food." Hippocrates used anise to cure coughs, a treatment still recommended today.

The ancient Druids also used plants in medicine, worship and spellcraft. For example, those who wanted to pass unnoticed used fern seeds for invisibility.

But with a vast array of healing and magical herbs available, where should the modern-day newbie witch begin? Why not start where your ancestors did: in your own backyard?

) THE FORAGER'S CODE (

Seeking out wild edibles feels very witchy but keep your sensible hat on. Getting snip-happy with plants you don't know can harm you and nature. So keep in mind these rules while you're out and about.

Remember plants are living things – obvious perhaps, but easy to forget in the thrill of the chase! So no matter how excited you are to discover a sought-after wild plant, tread softly and harvest gently. Use a blade to avoid damaging the rest of the plant and remember one flash of the secateurs too many and the plant may never recover.

Never forage a plant you can't identify with total certainty – most people are aware of the need to be careful with fungi but plants can be just as dangerous. For example, the medicinal yarrow looks almost identical to the deadly spotted water hemlock.

When foraging on someone else's land, ask permission first – you wouldn't take a bike from someone's garden without asking. The same goes for plants!

☽ NINE HERBS CHARM ☾

Old English herbalists foraged many native herbs and plants to brew potions and cast spells. One of the most intriguing herbal spells – the Nine Herbs Charm – is noted in a medical compilation, known as *Lacnunga*, which Anglo-Saxons recorded in the tenth century CE.

The tome details almost 200 remedies, prayers, blessings and charms for humans and livestock, combining Anglo-Saxon, British Pagan and Germanic folklore. The Nine Sacred Herbs Charm, which, according to Saxon beliefs, protected against disease, featured nine wild herbs. These included:

- Mayweed, most probably camomile (*Matricaria chamomilla*)
- Nettle (*Urtica dioica*)
- Fennel (*Foeniculum vulgare*)
- Crab apple (*Malus sylvestris*)
- Mugwort (*Artemisia vulgaris*)
- Broadleaf plantain (*Plantago major*)
- Hairy bittercress (*Cardamine hirsuta*)
- Chervil (*Anthriscus cerefolium*) or thyme (Thymus vulgaris)

- Cockspur grass (*Echinochloa crus-galli*) or betony (*Stachys officinalis*)

The herbs on their own are also very powerful, read on to learn more about these and others.

CAMOMILE

This hardy, self-seeding herb belongs to the daisy family. Look out for knee-high stems, a bright-gold centre and feathery white petals. Its name comes from the Greek *chamamelon*, meaning "apple on the ground" – when crushed, it releases an apple scent.

Healing and Witchcraft:

- Healers have historically used camomile to treat low appetite, bronchitis, worms and skin complaints.
- Camomile tea is a popular sleep aid and anxiety remedy.
- Witches plant it in their gardens to fortify their homes and use it in banishing rituals.
- Camomile brings luck in money-making spells.

NETTLE

This highly nutritious wonder weed thrives in fields, swamps, along roadsides, and on riverbanks from late spring to autumn. Watch out for the sting!

Healing and Witchcraft:

- The ancient Egyptians flogged themselves with nettle to relieve arthritis.
- Witches carry nettle sachets to ward off ghosts. Likewise, garden nettles banish evil spirits.
- Freshly cut nettle at the bedside soothes the sick.
- Polish witches use nettle smoke to chase away clouds.

FENNEL

Hardy perennial fennel has a liquorice scent, feathery leaves and yellow flowers. Although part of the carrot family, its name comes from the Old English word for "hay".

Healing and Witchcraft:

- Fennel seeds' sweet flavour curbs sugar cravings.
- It aids digestion and freshens the breath.

- Fennel is popular with breastfeeding mothers: it stimulates milk production and soothes colic.
- Witches chew fennel before important meetings to feel more confident, eloquent and persuasive.

CRAB APPLE

The crab apple is a wild ancestor of cultivated apple species now found all over the world. When an apple is sliced through the middle, the seeds form a pentagram, linking it to witchcraft.

Healing and Witchcraft:

- Bach Flower Remedies use crab apple to combat self-loathing, hopelessness and obsessions.
- To eliminate warts, folk healers rub them with apple slices, then bury the apple.
- Witches use apples at Samhain in spells to communicate with the dead.
- Apple wands are used in healing spells.

MUGWORT

An aromatic flowering plant, mugwort takes its Latin name – *Artemisia vulgaris* – from the Greek moon goddess, Artemis.

Healing and Witchcraft:

- Anglo-Saxons used mugwort to treat "elf shot" – a sickness inflicted by invisible arrows from fairies.
- *Bald's Leechbook* – a tenth-century medical text – recommends a mugwort remedy for demonic possession.
- In pre-Christian Britain, party-goers wore mugwort belts to the midsummer fire. These were ceremoniously burned at the night's end, averting evil forces for the coming year.
- Contemporary witches use mugwort incense to induce prophetic dreaming.

BROADLEAF PLANTAIN

This hardy, prolific perennial grows well in compacted soils, often appearing between stepping stones and pavement cracks. It is not closely related to the fruit with the same name.

Healing and Witchcraft:

- Nicknamed the "mother of all herbs", Anglo-Saxons used plantain to protect against colds and flu.
- Topically, it was used to treat skin complaints.
- Witches use plantain in spells and rituals for personal strength, protection and courage.

HAIRY BITTERCRESS

This evergreen perennial is a member of the Brassicaceae family. Its leaves and purple flowers have a delicious, peppery tang – perhaps explaining its name.

Healing and Witchcraft:

- In Saxon lore, hairy bittercress is said to drive out venom and remove pain.
- Hairy bittercress has diuretic, purgative and stimulating properties.
- It's thought to help with menstrual cramps.
- When placed under the bed, the intoxicating scent is believed to increase masculinity.

CHERVIL

Chervil once had a role in celebrations dedicated to Ceres, the goddess of grain and vegetation, which explains its Latin name – *Anthriscus cerefolium*. It's also known as French parsley.

Healing and Witchcraft:

- Chervil is a traditional remedy for weight loss.
- It was also thought to be a cure for hiccups and digestive complaints.
- Witches use chervil in rituals to contact the dead and in spells for wisdom.
- Folk magicians once boiled chervil with the highly poisonous pennyroyal to bring on altered states of consciousness.

THYME

This fragrant herb is a member of the mint family. Its low-growing woody stems boast clusters of pink-purple flowers in early summer.

Healing and Witchcraft:

- The thymol (a naturally occurring mixture of compounds) found in thyme leaves makes them a powerful antiseptic.

- Witches use thyme in money-drawing spells.
- Thyme sprigs were traditionally worn for courage – before a battle, ladies tied thyme to knights to increase their bravery.
- Mourners placed thyme on coffins to assure safe passage for the dead into the next life.

BETONY

Betony thrives on sunny banks and hedgerows, heathland and other grassy places. It's an indicator of ancient woodland.

Healing and Witchcraft:

- Traditionally, betony was seen as grounding and centring: a principal remedy for anxiety disorders.
- Traditional healers prescribed it for tension headaches and nervous digestion.
- Betony was planted in old churchyards to ward off unwelcome spirits.
- A Welsh charm recommends sleeping with betony leaves or drinking betony tea to prevent bad dreams.

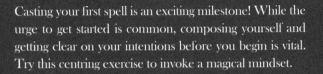

SPELLS AND RITUALS

Casting your first spell is an exciting milestone! While the urge to get started is common, composing yourself and getting clear on your intentions before you begin is vital. Try this centring exercise to invoke a magical mindset.

Begin by finding a peaceful spot outside. It doesn't have to be quiet, just somewhere safe where you won't be interrupted.

Take off your shoes and wiggle your toes in the earth. Tune into how the ground feels and imagine its energy infusing your body via your feet. If you're uncomfortable, you can put your shoes back on once you've established a connection.

Close your eyes and listen out for sounds: buzzing insects, rustling leaves or passing wildlife. Feel this energy enveloping you.

Repeat this exercise by observing sights and smells, imagining their energy filling your whole body.

DOS AND DON'TS OF SPELL CASTING

Do craft a positive intention. Focus on what you want to attract or manifest. For example, "I owe nothing and am financially free" is more positive than "I want to get rid of my debt", which focuses on the debt. Write the intention in the present tense and take in how it feels. If this is tricky, start with the phrase "I intend to be...".

Don't cast spells on others. While it's natural to yearn for control, white witchcraft is all about empowerment, so focus on yourself and leave others to follow their path. That doesn't mean you can't ask the universe to pave the way for your dreams and wishes!

Don't leave flames unattended; extinguish them safely once done. When burning herbs, light them with matches or a lighter and blow gently to nurture a glowing ember that gives off smoke. Keep a bowl of water nearby and submerge burning herbs to extinguish quickly if necessary.

☽ LOVE SPELLS ☾

A SPELL TO ATTRACT LOVE OR STRENGTHEN EXISTING BONDS

You will need:

- red or pink jewellery
- herbs of your choice
- matches
- romantic music
- candles

First, choose some jewellery: a piece including rose quartz – the crystal of love – is ideal, but any pink jewellery can magnetize a soulmate. If you're seeking passion, red jewellery conjures lust.

Next, cleanse and charge the item by passing it through the smoke of burning herbs. See the chapter on the power of herbs (page 58) for inspiration. Alternatively, a sprig of rosemary – a favourite of Aphrodite, the Greek goddess of love – or basil – the Roman herb of love, is perfect.

Next, purify your space and set the mood with candles and music. Then, holding your jewellery in both hands, visualize your wish. Want more alone time with your love? Picture a long, lazy afternoon, just the two of you, and let the warm glow of contentment infuse your jewellery.

Finally, slip on the jewellery, cinching the spell with an affirmative "and so it will be".

SEALED-WITH-A-KISS SPELL

This spell taps into ancient symbolism and the tradition of sealing letters with wax. It can rekindle the spark in tired relationships or help single witches form new bonds.

You will need:

- a pink or red candle
- matches
- attractive notepaper and an envelope
- a red pen

First, light your candle.

With your pen and notepaper, write a letter to your beloved as if your wish was already true. For example, if you wish for more laughter, you could write: "I love how much we laugh together."

When you feel loved-up, put the letter in the envelope.

Carefully hold your candle over the envelope flap so a few drops of melted wax drip to form a seal.

Allow the wax to cool and use the head of your match to inscribe it with the symbol "X". In Norse mythology, this "gebu" rune denotes love and partnership. It's also the modern-day symbol of a kiss.

Sleep with the letter under your pillow.

AN ENERGY-BURYING SPELL

Even loving partners experience moments of friction or gather resentments over time. Witchcraft can help you cast off any bad feeling so your relationship can move on with love. Cast this spell to release any ill feelings after a quarrel or to let go of lingering bitterness.

You will need:

- a hen's egg
- a bowl
- two small crystals – check out the chapter on crystals and gemstones (page 50) for inspiration. Alternatively, rose quartz is a good all-rounder. You will be sacrificing these crystals to the earth, so choose ones you're willing to part with
- a wand
- a trowel
- a calm spot in nature

Start by cracking your egg very carefully over the bowl. You're aiming to crack the shell into two parts that can fit back together. Catch the contents in the bowl and set aside.

Put one crystal inside each half of the egg shell and gently push the two halves back together to enclose the crystals.

Take the egg outside to your calm spot.

With an anticlockwise motion, use your wand to draw a circle in the soil roughly 10 cm (4 in.) wide.

Use the trowel to dig a hole in the centre of the circle, big enough to hold the egg.

Place the egg inside the circle and bury it with the soil.

Placing your hands on the earth above the egg, chant:

Spirit of earth, take this strife
Bring peace and harmony to my life.
Trouble, be gone,
So we can move on.
So mote it be.

Visualize the earth absorbing any negative feelings so two bright crystals are left in their place.

☽ **HAPPINESS SPELLS** ☾

A SPELL TO BRING JOY TO A FRIEND

You will need:

- a small bunch of cheerful flowers: yellow blooms symbolize happiness, so look for sunflowers, daffodils or yellow roses
- 30 cm (12 in.) yellow ribbon

Lay out your flowers, selecting only the healthiest stems.

Begin arranging them into a posy. Don't worry, this isn't about perfection. It's more about the positive vibes, so think happy thoughts. Reminisce on happy memories you've shared, or perhaps look back to a time when your friend seemed particularly content.

When you feel like you've conjured a happy vibe, wrap the ribbon around the stems. In your mind's eye hold on to an image of your friend smiling and laughing while chanting:

Flowers of earth, rain and sun,
Send happiness to my loved one.
With your beauty and sweet scent,
Help them feel so content.

Be sure to present your bouquet with both hands and a big smile.

A SPELL FOR PERSONAL HAPPINESS

Amp up the feel-good vibes with this spell for personal happiness that should be performed on the night of a full moon and close to a hawthorn tree. These small, dense, thorny trees or bushes are common in hedgerows. Celtic folklore states that hawthorns are witches who've transformed into trees. Their healing powers can benefit the heart emotionally and physically.

You will need:

- a piece of yellow cloth
- a cup of wine or moon water (see page 91) or a tablespoon of honey

To begin, on a night of a full moon, draw close to your hawthorn tree. Quietly sit beside it until you feel yourself attuning to its vibration. When you're ready, pierce a scrap of yellow cloth onto one of the tree's thorns, chanting:

Spirit of the hawthorn tree,
Bring happiness unto me.

Close the ritual by thanking the tree and sprinkling an offering of wine, honey or moon water at its roots.

A SPELL FOR BELONGING

Having a place to call home and feeling like you belong can do wonders for happiness. But sometimes, a space can feel unfamiliar, restless or just plain "meh". This ritual will clear any negativity from your building or room. It will also help you connect with the space and settle in, so it feels like home.

You will need:

- a handful of dried herbs, still on the stalk, that feel cleansing to you; vervain, rosemary and juniper are traditionally used for house cleansing (alternatively, check out the chapter on the power of herbs for inspiration, see page 58)
- 30 cm (12 in.) natural twine
- matches
- a feather

First, fashion your stalks into a bunch and secure them with the twine.

Light the herbs with the matches or a lighter and blow on them to nurture a glowing ember that gives off smoke. You may have to repeat this a few times throughout the ritual to keep the herbs burning.

Walk around your house or room holding your burning herbs, wafting the smoke with the feather. Encourage the smoke into all corners, top and bottom.

As you walk, say this incantation:

> ***Bless this house,***
> ***From above and below,***
> ***Hidden corners, places that show,***
> ***Top to bottom, end to end,***
> ***Under, over, around every bend.***

The space is now clear, full of positive energy and should smell beautifully. Repeat regularly to nurture a positive atmosphere.

☽ SUCCESS SPELLS ☾

CREATE A WITCH'S LADDER

Also known as a rope-and-feathers spell, a witch's ladder is made of knotted cord. It's a tradition for witches to spend time mindfully knotting cords while contemplating specific magical intentions. The number of knots and charms varies according to the intended effect.

Like prayer beads or a rosary, rituals such as this have a wide-ranging spiritual history. Knotting the cord while chanting focuses the mind and intensifies intentions.

When completed, a witch's ladder can also act as a counting aid. Certain spells require multiple repetitions of incantations or actions. Witches use the ladder to track their count, running the feathers or beads through their hands as they go.

The first record of a witch's ladder was discovered in 1875, when workmen were demolishing an old house in Wellington, Somerset. The attic hid six broomsticks, an old armchair and a long piece of cord knotted with chicken feathers.

Try this witch's ladder spell to bring about your ambition.

You will need:

- 50 cm (20 in.) cord in any colour – golden thread is ideal as it symbolizes success
- beads, charms or feathers that represent your wish
- candles and incense
- matches

To begin the ritual, light candles and incense and centre yourself.

Begin tying knots in the sequence below and threading the charms when you feel called to do so while chanting:

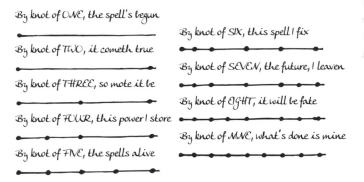

By knot of ONE, the spell's begun

By knot of TWO, it cometh true

By knot of THREE, so mote it be

By knot of FOUR, this power I store

By knot of FIVE, the spells alive

By knot of SIX, this spell I fix

By knot of SEVEN, the future, I leaven

By knot of EIGHT, it will be fate

By knot of NINE, what's done is mine

EMAIL YOURSELF SUCCESS

Email spells are discreet, quick and easy. Yet, there's something conclusive about hitting send – like ticking off something on your to-do list.

All you need is access to an email account.

Find a moment to yourself and decide on your intention for the spell. When you're ready, create a brand-new message in your email account, addressed to yourself. In the subject box, write a positive headline, "Well done!" or "Great News!" perhaps.

Write your intention into the body of the email. It doesn't have to be long or complicated. Write it as if your wish was already true or the desired result had already happened. For example, "Well done on that great presentation today, Sarah. You came across as a safe pair of hands."

Hit send on the email and log out immediately.

Leave the email unread until it comes true. Then view and delete the message.

A CANDLE SPELL TO PREDICT SUCCESS

Do you have an important decision looming? This candle spell will identify the most successful option for you. Perform it at night in a quiet, dark room.

You will need:

- a candle
- matches
- a yes/no question

Wait for nightfall, then find a dark room where you won't be interrupted.

To begin, light the candle and let it burn for a few moments, so the flame settles.

When you're ready, draw close to the candle, within breath's reach. Ask the candle your question in your normal speaking voice. Be sure to phrase it so the answer is yes or no.

Watch the flame. If it jumps, grows or sizzles as if it's growing in energy, the answer is yes. However, if it dips or flickers, as if losing power, or even goes out, the answer is no. If sparks fly, the outcome is beyond your control, no matter what you decide.

Extinguish your candle when done.

☽ PROTECTION SPELLS ☾

AN APPLE SPELL FOR PROTECTION

This simple apple spell invokes the protection of a pentagram, which was a powerful symbol in ancient times. Despite being misinterpreted as a sign of dark magick, many religions and organizations have used it historically, including Christianity and the Freemasons.

Tradition says the star's five points represent the union of the spirit and the four elements: earth, water, fire and air. Other representations for the five points include the five senses, the five fingers, the five wounds of Christ and the five planets: Saturn, Jupiter, Mars, Mercury and Venus.

Today, many Wiccans wear pentagrams as symbols of their beliefs. For them, an upright pentagram represents the triumph of spirit over matter. In addition, pentagrams are often used in magic to summon or banish elemental energies and provide protection.

You will need:

- an apple
- a knife
- ten whole clove buds
- a dinner plate

- salt
- a black candle

Before you begin, cut an apple horizontally to reveal the pentagram-shaped seeds.

PIERCE 1 CLOVE INTO THE APPLE FLESH NEAR EACH OF THESE POINTS

Next, in each of the apple halves, push the clove buds into the flesh of the apple near the five points of the pentagram.

Sprinkle a ring of salt around your plate.

Place the clove-studded apple halves in the middle of the plate.

Hold the black candle and visualize protective energy infusing the wax.

Light the candle, securing it between the apple halves in a holder or with melted wax.

Watch the candle burn for as long as you wish, allowing the protective glow to bring you peace of mind.

A FEATHER AMULET FOR PROTECTION

Feathers represent communication, freedom and flight. Use a found feather to create an amulet to ask for protection and freedom from worry. Depending on your leanings, you can ask deities, spirits or the energy of the universe.

You will need:

- a few feathers found in nature; white feathers symbolize spiritual connection and protection
- a small drawstring bag
- a passport-sized photograph of your loved one or other trinkets that inspire a sense of safety for you; you can even draw symbols on small pieces of paper if that helps

Gather the feathers and other trinkets.

Begin mindfully placing them inside the bag, drawing to mind what they mean to you. For example:

This feather brings me freedom from worry.

This trinket channels my grandfather's protection.

Once you've filled your bag, you can carry it in your purse, pin it inside your coat or sleep with it under your pillow.

PROTECTION FROM THE EVIL EYE

According to Italian folklore, the "evil eye" – or *il malocchio* – is everywhere. Symptoms of being caught in its gaze include brain fog, ill health, bad luck and financial ruin. Luckily, there's a simple cure.

You will need:

- a white bowl filled with 500 ml (1 pint) water
- 50 ml (3 tbsp) olive oil
- scissors
- two garlic bulbs

Begin by dripping oil off your pinky finger into the water, watching what happens.

If the oil scatters, you're all good. But if it gathers into a glob – or eye – the evil eye is upon you.

Break the curse with a prayer for release while snipping the scissors over the bowl.

Test the spell has worked by repeating the above, using fresh water and oil. Repeat as necessary.

As soon as you're free, hang the garlic at your front and back doors.

) FORTUNE-TELLING SPELLS (

Are you facing a decision? Why not try asking a pendulum? A pendulum is a weight attached to a string or chain. They are so named because, when held weight-down, they pendulate, or swing.

A pendulum isn't a new-age fad; the ancient Egyptians and Romans favoured them for divination and dowsing, but their use probably pre-dates written records. Galileo Galilei was the first to study pendulums formally in 1602. They also captured the imaginations of Leonardo da Vinci, Isaac Newton, Albert Einstein and Thomas Edison.

Witches use pendulums to find things, answer questions and see the future. First, they hold the pendulum steady – weight down – before asking a yes/no question. Then, when the pendulum

begins to swing, they interpret the answer based on pre-agreed criteria. They use a similar method to find minerals, underground water, lost objects or people by holding the pendulum over a map and letting it swing over significant locations.

PENDULUM DOWSING

Pendulum dowsing is an easy divination method – no psychic abilities or special equipment are necessary.

You will need:

- a weight (try a crystal or ring)
- 25 cm (10 in.) chain or string

Although you can buy ready-made pendulums, making your own can allow you to channel the wisdom of an ancestor, using an heirloom ring, or harness the properties of a particular crystal. Simply take your chosen weight and thread it onto a chain or string.

Cleanse the pendulum by leaving it in fresh water or moonlight overnight. Skip this step if you're channelling the previous owner.

Next, discover how your pendulum communicates. Hold it steady, weight-down, asking, "show me a yes". Note the direction of its swing. Repeat with "no" and "maybe" instructions. Once you're confident, ask the pendulum a more significant question.

Some believe pendulums work by connecting with divine forces. For others, the swing is down to involuntary muscle movements that channel the higher self.

BLACK MIRROR SCRYING

Scrying – also known as seeing or peeping – is the process of peering into a suitable medium to see messages or visions about the future.

Traditionally, witches used a cauldron of water or a black mirror. However, this method uses the screen on your phone or tablet in moments when it's turned off. This portal into your subconscious will bring hidden visions into the light.

You will need:

- a smartphone or tablet
- a soft cloth
- four tea-light candles

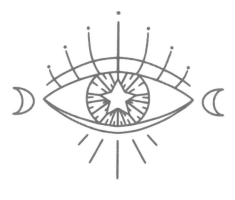

Choose a quiet spot at night and begin by turning off your device completely and cleaning it with the soft cloth. Next, perform an energetic cleanse by imagining the device becoming enveloped in pure, white light.

Cast a circle by surrounding the device with the four candles, one at each compass point. Extinguish other sources of light.

Clear your mind and soften your gaze on the screen, which will now act as a black mirror.

Let images appear on the screen or in your mind's eye. This process can take time and practice, so be patient. It's common to see wispy shapes or vague outlines. Others will see more vivid images.

Practise for around 15 minutes, then close the ritual by imagining a white light encircling you.

Make a note of your visions and consider how you might interpret them.

❭ MOON RITUALS ❬

Lunar energy can add zing to your spell-work. Timing your spells with the phases of the moon is like swimming with the tide: it's much easier and more effective.

The new moon promotes new beginnings – amplifying spells focused on a new job, relationship or house – while a waxing moon attracts or increases things, so spells focused on wealth and success will benefit.

A full moon boosts manifestation spells. These spells involve the Law of Attraction, which asserts that the universe acts like a giant echo chamber, reflecting your thoughts, feelings and beliefs in what's possible. Any spells involving appreciation, affirmation or visualization, which create positivity, will manifest more quickly at this time.

A waning moon repels or decreases things and shines light elsewhere. So it's particularly suited to spells aimed

at letting go. Or perhaps you want to beam your spell-work toward others? Don't forget to ask permission first!

MOON WATER

Water is receptive: imbuing water with moonlight harnesses the power of the moon. Keep tabs on the moon phases if you have an intention in mind and time your ritual accordingly.

You will need:

- a container – a glass preserving jar with a clear lid works best
- a source of natural water – such as a river, spring or the ocean. You can also collect rainwater. If you want to drink the moon water, use bottled spring water
- sage leaves – or choose herbs that compliment your intention if possible. (See The Power of Herbs, page 58, for inspiration)
- matches

First, cleanse a container by holding it in the smoke of the burning herbs.

Pour your water into the container.

Leave the water outside overnight, in clear view of the moon.

The next day, use the water in your spell-work. Alternatively, use it to cleanse or anoint yourself, your magical tools or your home.

A RITUAL MOON BATH

Harness the releasing power of the dark moon during the final phase of the lunar cycle – around day 28 when the lack of solar reflection renders the moon's face dark. As the moon completes its cycle and slides out of view, it's an opportune time to let go of anything that no longer serves you.

On the night of the dark moon, run a candle-lit bath, imagining it's a giant cauldron in your bathroom. Add to the atmosphere by leaving a window open if possible. Don't worry; you won't see the moon during this phase, but the energy is still potent.

Add a slosh of moon water if you have any.

Lie in the water, imagining cleansing moonbeams washing away that which no longer serves you. Bask in their silvery glow. Now is the perfect time to let go of fears, resentments, prejudices or negativity, ready to start a new phase.

Then, as the water drains out, imagine your troubles disappearing too.

A FULL MOON ENERGY BOOST

A full moon brings energy and power. With the sun and moon aligned on either side of the earth, we're blessed with an uninterrupted view of the moon's face. It's an opportunity to align yourself with the moon's power to increase your energy.

You will need:

- uplifting music that suits your intention
- a clear space where you can dance uninterrupted

On a night with a full moon, take a bracing shower. Turn down the temperature, if you dare, or boost circulation with a good scrub.

Quickly dry yourself while your skin is still tingling, lower the lights and turn on your music. Clothes are optional: enjoy being naked if you feel comfortable. If not, dress in comfy clothes or something that feels beautiful.

Feel the music's rhythm vibrating through your body, the melody filling your heart, the tune pulling you along. Close your eyes, visualize the moon beams filling your body and let go!

Sing along or chant an uplifting mantra for extra power.

☽ MANIFESTATION ☾

A SHAMBLE FOR MANIFESTATION

A shamble is a tool to magnify the power of your intention, which helps manifestation. It sounds like a mess, and in a way it is! It looks like a dream catcher, a mobile or a tattered spider's web tangled with treasures.

The shamble isn't magical in itself; it's a tool that enables a witch to see more clearly, sharpen her focus and communicate intentions to the universe.

You will need:

- anything and everything – that's the point of a shamble. It's an artful arrangement of things you happen to come across: include a mixture of natural and personal objects – these don't have to be meaningful – odds and ends from your pocket, garden or local park will do
- one live ingredient – this is the only must-have. Choose a bud, seed or even a beetle (don't worry, the shamble won't harm it)
- a ball of string or twine
- several sticks or strong twigs
- an intention you'd like to manifest

For extra potency, collect ingredients from a place that's special to you. Think windfall twigs, leaves, feathers and odds and ends you find in your pockets or on the ground. Don't be precious; trust what the universe is trying to bring to your attention.

Create a simple frame by securing the twigs with twine.

Weave a long piece of twine between the edges of the frame to form a rough net or hanging strings.

Next, attach your found objects using extra pieces of twine. As you do so, take in the properties of each piece with all your senses. Think about how they could relate to your purpose – perhaps the fallen leaves are a reminder to let go. Or a round stone could be a prompt to roll with what lies ahead. A penny could signify investment.

When your shamble feels complete, place the living element in the centre. Then, hang the shamble from a tree like a message to the universe.

TAKE AN ABUNDANCE BATH

Traditionally, witches harvest ingredients for prosperity spells during autumn. But you can enjoy this ritual to manifest prosperity anytime!

You will need:

- a saucepan and stove
- a cinnamon stick
- 5 dried clove buds
- 5 star anise pods
- a tablespoon of coconut oil
- a colander
- a green, gold or silver candle
- matches
- a pen
- a bay leaf
- a heatproof bowl
- 750 ml (1.5 pints) of water

Place the saucepan over a medium heat on the stovetop, add the water and spices and bring to a simmer. Strain and stir the potion into a hot bath with the coconut oil. Light your candle.

Write an intention relating to abundance on a bay leaf.

Then, hold your bay leaf over the candle flame, so the smoke releases your intention into the universe. (Keep the heatproof bowl nearby to dispose of the flaming leaf.)

Climb into your candle-lit bath and soak up the abundance.

QUICK-FIRE MANIFESTATION TECHNIQUES

- Just like when sunlight amplifies a mirror's reflection, mirrors amplify spells too. To increase the power of an intention, speak it into a mirror with conviction. Feel the power doubling and look forward to your intention manifesting.

- Did you know bells have powerful transformative energy? They often signify change. So next time you're saying affirmations, ring a bell in time with your chanting to call in positive, energetic influences and open new pathways.

- Blowing bubbles may seem like child's play, but have you noticed how they captivate everyone who sees them? Harness this magical quality in a manifestation ritual:

  - Sit with a pot of bubble mixture in your hands, close your eyes and focus on a dream in vivid detail.

  - Take the bubble mixture outside and begin blowing bubbles.

  - With every exhale, imagine the bubbles filling with your wish.

  - As they sail off and pop, the dream releases into the universe.

PRACTICAL MAGIC

For the newbie witch, the world of magic can feel like a far-off fairy tale, cloaked in mystery and ritual. After all, much of the daily grind feels far removed from magic, not to mention our society's preoccupation with materialistic and scientific thinking. Beginner witches may feel that the magical life is unobtainable or reserved for special occasions, but this couldn't be further from the truth.

Magick was a routine part of life for witches of old, with no need for elaborate rituals, aligning stars or full moons. Instead, traditional witches used simple ingredients and tools to improve everyday life.

If you find yourself wanting to infuse your life with more magic, it's not about sourcing exotic herbs and expensive crystals or hosting elaborate rituals once in a blue moon. Instead, it's about mastering the basics, so you're ready to turn your hand to witchcraft at any time. Read on to discover three practices that, once accomplished, will help you sprinkle magic through daily life.

☽ CREATE AN ALTAR ☾

Simply put, an altar is both a magical workstation and sanctuary: a space that's clean, ready and inspiring for witchcraft and reflection.

Primarily, it's a functional space, so stock it with tools and ingredients you regularly use: candles, matches, cleansing herbs, dishes for offerings and images of any deities or spirits you hold dear.

An altar should also be beautiful, so consider decorating yours with sentimental treasures. Or perhaps you'd like to pay homage to the seasons or the phases of the cosmos.

Your altar can also reflect your path and calling. For example, if you'd like to connect with the angels, why not include a white feather? Looking for love? Display rose quartz. Need to draw strength? Include an acorn or oak leaf.

Altars can be inside or out, elaborate or simple, temporary or permanent, hidden away or sitting proud. What's vital is the time and respect you devote to them. The more you invest, the more evocative your altar will become.

☽ CAST A CIRCLE ☾

This ritual quickly protects and elevates any space – perfect for when you're meditating or spell casting. If you have time, cleanse the air by burning herbs of your choice. Next, create a ring of protection by "calling the quarters".

Turn to the north quarter of your circle, saying, "I call upon the watchtowers of north and earth." Bring in earth symbols if you wish, such as soil or salt or a green candle.

Next, move to the east, saying, "I invite the gatekeepers of the east and air." Burn some incense, if you have any, to symbolize air.

Next, move to the south, saying, "I call upon the guardians of the south and fire." Light a red candle if you wish.

Finally, move to the west, saying, "I call upon the energy of the west and water." Sprinkle the air with water if you have any to hand.

Finish the ritual by bowing to each direction, saying, "May the directions and elements protect and balance this space. Thank you."

☽ CHARGE ITEMS ☾

Do you have a lucky charm or amulet? You've likely infused it with positive energy subconsciously! Objects gather energetic impressions from their owners and the environment. To charge an item is to do this intentionally and for a specific purpose. Why not charge your jewellery or magical tools?

The first step is to cleanse the item to remove accumulated energy. One method is to immerse it in natural running water or smoke. Alternatively, leave it outside under a full moon or in a dish of salt.

Next, create a sacred space, perhaps at your altar, with candles and incense and call in any spiritual helpers – for example, if you want luck in love, you could invite the love goddesses, Aphrodite and Venus, or ask the elements for support.

Finally, when you're ready, hold the item and meditate or chant on its purpose for a few moments. Imagine your wish is a reality and visualize this energy infusing your object. Tada! You've now enchanted the object with magical energy, so use it wisely!

) CULTIVATE GRATITUDE (

Gratitude helps swing the Law of Attraction in our favour. The below gratitude practice acts as a success magnet for all other spells, while feeling like a self-care ritual.

You will need:

- six bay leaves (or make your own leaves from green paper)
- a pen or permanent marker
- a green tea-light candle
- a green bowl or jar

Smooth out your leaves.

Light your green candle and focus on the flame for a few moments.

On each leaf, write a few words that call to mind a recent happening that made you feel grateful. It needs to be specific. So rather than thinking, "I'm grateful for my dog," think, "I'm grateful my dog greeted me with a waggy tail when I came home from work today."

When you've filled all your leaves, pick up each in turn and place it in your bowl, saying thank you as you do so.

When you're done, blow out the candle, but leave the bowl of leaves in view. They'll serve as a reminder of your blessings every time you see them.

KEEP A GRIMOIRE
OR BOOK OF SHADOWS

A grimoire is a manual detailing information that could be valuable to any witch. It includes practical instructions on summoning spirits, conducting spells, rituals and divinations, and creating amulets, talismans and charms. Some witches believe the books themselves are charged with magic. Many witches hand down grimoires through generations. Archaeologists have found grimoires detailing magical incantations dating back to the fifth and fourth centuries BCE.

The first *Book of Shadows* was penned by Gerald Gardner in the late 1940s or early 1950s. It's considered a religious text by Wiccans. The book began life as a shared text, kept by the high priestess or priest of a coven, but during the 1970s, when solitary non-initiatory witchcraft grew, witches began creating their own copies. Nowadays, a book of shadows is more often a personal journal – a shadow of its owner, perhaps. Why not start writing your own?

SPELLS FOR THE MODERN WORLD

The rich history of witchcraft is part of its attraction, but that doesn't mean it's backward-looking: witches have always been shapeshifters who move with the times.

Today that means embracing modern technology and media. That's how many recruits discover the craft. So it follows that the contemporary witch's toolkit includes devices alongside ancient crystals and traditional herbs.

Some take this further, believing technology itself is spiritual. In technopaganism, phones, cars, computers and the like have spirits and energy. After all, devices are an extension of the self for many, processing their every thought, feeling, desire and curiosity. So why wouldn't they absorb this energy?

Not keen on swapping your crystal for a phone? Maybe you don't have to. Did you know modern technology often uses quartz crystals thanks to their ability to convert mechanical energy into electricity and vice versa? So next time you use tech in your practice, know you're tapping into an ancient power too.

Read on to discover more witchy ways to incorporate tech into your practice.

❯ TECHNOLOGICAL SUPPORT ❮

Ancient craft and modern technology may not seem like a natural fit, but a new generation of witches are bringing witchcraft into the twenty-first century.

A VIRTUAL COVEN

Social media can help newbie witches come out of the shadows and tap into a witchy community. Witches use hashtags such as #witchtok and #witchesofinstagram to connect with like-minded souls.

AN ONLINE WITCHOPEDIA

Online tools reveal the magic in the world around you. Plant identification apps can help you forage on the fly while apps tracking the lunar calendar can help you understand cosmic influences in your location.

PRACTICAL SHORTCUTS

Candlelight and cauldrons are fantastic, but don't be shy about whipping out the torch or compass on your phone when spell casting outside. Likewise, your phone's notebook makes a perfect book of shadows for an on-the-go spiritualist.

) TECHNOLOGY SPELLS (

Spell casting should be accessible to all, but what if your landlord doesn't allow candles, or you can't afford crystals? Try making magic using virtual tools!

MAKE A WISH VIA TEXT

Don't have your wand handy? Send the universe a text instead:

- Create a message on your phone addressed to yourself.
- Spell out your wish in the present tense.
- Imagine what you want is already true, soaking up how that feels.
- Hit send, releasing the message into the universe.

Don't open the message yet; let the notification be a reminder of your wish every time you reach for your phone.

EMAIL DIVINATION

Emails can be a source of e-divination – next time you have a question, open an email you feel drawn to and scan for instructions. Read between the lines and use your imagination if necessary. You might be surprised at what the universe reveals.

❯ EMOJI SIGILS ❮

In traditional witchcraft, witches create visual representations of spells using sigils (see also page 117). These pictures combine symbols, colours and codes in artistic and experimental ways – much like emojis.

Emoji sigils can be unique to their creator and each spell or used collectively. Some witches share them on social media, believing every "like" or "share" adds power. So why not create your own?

Firstly, state your desire as if it were already true. "I am paid well for work I love," rather than "I want more money," for example.

Choose emojis to represent your wish. Get creative; it's OK to be cryptic if the meaning is clear to you. To create a sacred space, bookend each sigil with a magical emoji, such as a candle or crystal ball and focus on your wish. Here are some ideas:

I'm confident at public speaking!

I'll get well soon!

Release your emoji sigil into the universe via text message or social media.

HOW TO DEVISE YOUR OWN SPELLS, RITUALS AND CHANTS

Other people's spells are a helpful way into witchcraft – the spells in this book are a useful starting point – but, likely, you'll soon want to devise your own. After all, witchcraft is all about self-empowerment, channelling your ability to create what you want is the whole point. Got itchy fingers? Believe in yourself and go for it.

Don't worry; there's no need to feel daunted: even the simplest tools and formulas become very powerful when you put your unique spin on them. This chapter will look at the natural forces you can call on in spell making. You'll learn how to channel the energy of moon phases, deities and the weather, and how to create your own symbols and chants. Finally, get your magic on by using our spell template.

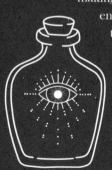

But first, a reminder about personalizing your goal for maximum success.

) DEFINING YOUR DREAMS (

Deciding what you want is fundamental to any spell. By now, you'll know that vague ideas won't cut it. True transformation requires details. Define your dream in clear, positive terms, using the present tense.

Another tip is to focus on internal rather than external desires: "I get a promotion" becomes "I feel fully expressed at work" for instance – because true fulfilment always comes from within.

For extra power, focus on how your dream serves others and aligns with the best outcomes for all. For example, "I retrain as a nutritionist and help people lead healthier lives." Gabby Bernstein calls this the "Spiritually Aligned Action Method", commenting, "When you align your energy with service and inspiration, you can trust that it will propel your vision forward."

A note on self-doubt: feeling like you're undeserving or not up to the challenge puts the brakes on magical momentum. So do whatever you need to boost your self-belief before you start.

☽ HARNESSING THE MOON ☾

Now you're clear on your goal, let's look at the optimal timing of your spell. One way of doing this is by harnessing the energy of the moon.

We've already touched on how the moon has always had powerful significance for witches. Let's expand by tailoring your spells to channel the moon's magical force here.

NEW MOON: NEW BEGINNINGS

The new moon represents positive change and new beginnings. It's a good time for spells about new jobs or businesses, moving house or fertility.

WAXING MOON: GROWTH

The waxing moon represents growth. Therefore, it lends itself to attraction spells – those looking to draw more love, wealth or health.

FULL MOON: FULL POWER

Energy and emotion intensify during a full moon, so it's the most potent time for magic. Many witches also feel heightened psychic ability, so trust your instincts.

WANING MOON: REPELLING AND LETTING GO

As the moon recedes in the night sky, it's an ideal time to seek liberation. Let go of regret, resentments, old flames or negative relationships.

DARK MOON: INTROSPECTION

When the moon disappears in the three days before a new moon, it's a time for reflection and listening to your inner voice. Divination work is particularly revealing at this time.

LUNAR ECLIPSE: REMOVING OBSTACLES AND GROWTH

When the earth passes between the sun and a full moon, it creates a lunar eclipse. Historically, many cultures have seen them as harbingers of doom. However, they can encourage growth. Also, because eclipses appear to show the moon moving through all its phases, they're helpful for creating a sense of momentum and change.

SOLAR ECLIPSE: REBIRTH

These occur when the moon passes between the sun and the earth during the new moon phase. Some witches believe the eclipse is a power blocker; for others, it's time for spiritual rebirth.

) HARNESSING THE DIVINE (

Bring a divine touch to your practice by working with personal deities. Connecting with gods and goddesses is all about your intuition and natural leanings. If you don't know where to start, why not:

- Consider any pantheons you admire.
- Research how deities are valued and ritualized in those cultures.
- Immerse yourself in the interests, stories and values of deities you admire.
- Evaluate what they could add to your practice and consider a regular commitment. Be wary of long-term oaths; your needs and interests will change over time. If you don't warm to a deity, thank them and move on.

When you find a deity you want to work with, consider:

- Inviting them to rituals and celebrations on a spiritual level.
- Asking them to draw close during meditation.
- Learning about them through creative projects.
- Honouring them with offerings, prayers or devotion to a relevant cause.

Once you've established a bond, feel free to ask your deity to help with your spell-work.

☽ POPULAR DEITIES ☾
IN WITCHCRAFT

Paganism and Wicca worship the divine using masculine, feminine and gender-neutral imagery. The god and goddess deities are the most well-known: their conception, birth and death cycle shape the year.

THE TRIPLE GODDESS

The Triple Goddess has three forms: maiden, mother and crone. The maiden relates to the waxing crescent moon, the mother to the full moon and the crone to the waning crescent. Having no assigned face, the goddess appears differently in many pantheons.

- In Greek mythology, the moon goddess Hecate appears in three aspects.
- In Roman mythology, the moon goddess Diana takes three forms.
- In Norse mythology, the Triple Goddess appears in the three Norns.
- In Celtic mythology, the Triple Goddess presents as three sisters.
- In the ancient Near East, Qudshu-Astarte-Anat is a single goddess who combines three goddesses.

THE HORNED GOD

The Triple Goddess' counterpart is the Horned God. His two horns symbolize his dual nature, combining light and dark and the union of the divine and the animal. He is known by many names:

- As the woodland deity of Arcadia, the ancient Greeks called him Pan.
- In English folklore, he appears as Herne, the hunter of rural England.
- In Celtic traditions he's represented by the "Oak King" and "Holly King".
- In Gallo Roman religion, he's known as Cernunnos.

There's a deity for everyone. Wicca and witchcraft have always celebrated "otherness", with many branches looking beyond gender-binary idols. In his 1978 book *Witchcraft and the Gay Counterculture*, Arthur Evans re-evaluates religious figures such as Joan of Arc, believing she was transgender or a cross-dressing lesbian.

) WORKING WITH THE WEATHER (

We experience the energy of the weather through all our senses: the boom of thunder, the nip of a cold autumn day, the light and shade of clouds skidding over the sun. The weather affects our moods, daily routines and lifestyles. But did you know it's possible to harness this energy to enhance your spells?

- Heavy rain washes away negativity, enhancing healing and cleansing spells.
- Snow and ice are fleeting and purifying, so enhance spells that aim to get rid of things. Scrape your wish into an icy surface and watch it melt away.
- Cloud patterns can reveal messages and divine the future.
- Wind brings a sense of movement; great for change, sending messages or directing energy. Wind directions also have specific powers.
  - The north wind enhances spells involving a past action or incident.
  - The south wind brings energy and passion and forward momentum.
  - The east wind guides intuition and new beginnings.
  - The west wind brings love, fertility and creativity.

☽ **WRITING INCANTATIONS AND CHANTS** ☾

Words have incredible power, whether carefully considered or remarked offhand, so it makes sense that spells often include them in the form of incantations and chants. Writing your own is even more meaningful.

One easy method is to break the verse into three parts: what you want, when you want it and the desired result. Here are some examples:

> *Tonight I'm blessed*
> *With peace and rest,*
> *And so tomorrow,*
> *I feel my best.*

> *As I make my speech today*
> *All my nerves melt away*
> *And listeners heed what I say.*

Using rhyming words makes incantations easier to remember and brings rhythmical energy. But don't worry if you're not a poet; let go of your inhibitions and let your imagination riff. You're only writing for yourself.

) WORKING WITH (MAGICAL SIGILS

Sigils are symbols that hold magical or mystical meanings. From the Latin *sigillum*, which means "seal", sigil is the root of many other English words like signature, sign and signal.

Historically, magicians believed sigils were the pictorial signatures of supernatural entities. Witches thought sigils gave them an element of control over angels, demons and spirits.

These days, witches use the word to refer to magical intentions they've condensed into a single graphic. The theory goes that creating a sigil triggers creativity and visualization, thus prompting the subconscious to look for ways to manifest goals.

Unique to their creators and often kept secret, sigils are a way to voice a wish to the universe while maintaining privacy. Earlier we looked at how emojis can be used to create a sigil (see page 107) but now it's time to learn how to draw your own. Read on to learn an easy method.

☽ HOW TO CREATE A SIGIL ☾

Write your wish or intention in the present tense, using positive language as if it were already true. For example:

I speak my truth

Pick out the key word. For example, "truth".

Look at the letters and remove any duplicates and vowels. For example, in this case, we're left with:

T R H

Combine these to create a single glyph. You can be creative with this by breaking down letters into different strokes and laying letters on top of each other. For example:

Now you need to give the sigil energy by activating or charging it. There are lots of methods but the simplest uses visualization.

Draw your sigil and place your hands over it, imagining your wish is a reality. Visualize this feeling infusing the sigil.

Now you're ready to release your sigil into the universe! Let your imagination run wild:

- Draw it on the sand and let the sea wash it away.
- Draw it in the air and walk through it.
- Draw it in dust, then blow it away.
- Draw it on food, then eat it.
- Draw it on firewood, then burn it.
- Draw it on a balloon, then pop it.
- Draw it on your body and wash it away in a ritual bath.
- Draw it on a rock and throw it into a body of water.
- Draw it on condensation, then allow it to disappear.
- Engrave it on jewellery.
- Scrape it into the earth, then stamp on it.
- Inscribe it on the soles of shoes.

☽ CREATING CUSTOM SPELLS, STEP BY STEP ☾

DEFINE YOUR INTENTION OR PURPOSE

- Write it down and finesse the wording to get it just right.
- Choose and gather your magical tools: wand/cauldron/candle/etc.
- Choose and gather your magical ingredients: herbs/crystals/found objects/etc.

DRAW ON MAGICAL ENERGY

- Decide what timing best serves your intention: moon phase/during certain weather conditions/before a particular event.
- Decide what setting best serves your intention: indoor/outdoor/at an altar/at a specific place.
- Optional: decide what energetic support best serves your intention: deities/spirits/elemental forces.

COMBINE

- How could you use your magical tools and magical ingredients to conjure your desired result?

- How could you amplify the effect with magical energy?
- Start simple, you can add flourish in the next stage.

FINESSE WITH FINAL TOUCHES

- What words could bring the spell together?
- How can you add a sense of ritual? With incense/ music/ceremony?
- Do you need any other props?

PRACTISE

- Run through individual elements to perfect the flow.

EXECUTE

- Perform the spell.

REVIEW

- Record any observations and ideas for future tweaks after you've performed the spell.

JOIN A COVEN OR PRACTISE SOLO

If you've been reading up on witchcraft, conjuring a few spells and perhaps even following seasonal rituals, you're likely feeling fired up about the magical path. Depending on your leanings, many witches feel called to seek out like-minded witches at this point. There's nothing like the shared wonder of a well-cast spell to get the cauldron bubbling.

But how do you know if you're ready to join a coven? And if a witchy fellowship is for you, where do you look? If only you could conjure up a wise witch elder who could take you under her cloak and lead you into the fold.

High priestess manifestations aside, a more realistic approach is to put out feelers and ask around to discover what's out there. Like-minded souls and potential covens might not be in plain sight, but once you start looking, you'll find a vast and varied magical realm.

Read on to discover questions you should ask yourself, and potential coven mates, before taking your place around the cauldron.

HOW BEST TO
APPROACH A LOCAL COVEN

If you're looking for a Wiccan coven or other like-minded group, start exploring your local witchy scene.

Many witches are still in the broom closet. Yet psychic fairs, spiritual events, alternative coffee shops and even book shops can be fertile ground for discovery.

When you find a group, it's time for some soul searching. Before committing, ask yourself:

- Who does the group welcome and will you fit?
- Do they have a purpose and does it align with yours?
- Are you comfortable with any deities they follow?
- Are you comfortable with the hierarchy, rules and guidelines?
- Is the schedule convenient?
- Is there any cost involved?
- What seasonal rituals does the group celebrate?
- Is it an inspiring place to learn and grow?
- What happens if you decide it's not for you?

Be patient if you don't find fellowship immediately; keep searching or start your own coven. Alternatively, many witches find fulfilment on their own – white witchcraft is all about self-empowerment after all. You are enough.

☽ FINAL WORD ☾

Did you connect with the moon or harness the power of the weather while reading this book? Exploring the craft may have brought you closer to the seasons. Are you seeing your surroundings through a more magical lens now?

Or maybe witchcraft has lit your creative spark: have you composed a sigil, whipped up a herbal remedy or penned an incantation?

Or perhaps, for you, this book has been an invitation for self-care. Hopefully, you've wallowed in a ritual bath, scribbled secrets in your book of shadows or indulged in mindfulness.

The craft may have opened your eyes to new dimensions: have you developed a connection with deities or found a sense of belonging by joining a coven? Maybe celebrating seasonal rhythms has illuminated the cyclical nature of life. After all, just as the Wheel of the Year turns, birth, growth, maturity, death and rebirth are part of human existence.

It doesn't matter whether you've gone "full witch" or merely peeked under the veil. The magical path is always open. So come as you are, when you're ready, and you'll find self-empowerment, self-expression and self-care along the way.

Do you believe in witchcraft? Because it believes in you.

GLOSSARY

Black magick – Magick that invokes evil spirits for evil ends.

Charge – The act of filling something with energy or purpose.

Circle – In witchcraft, a "circle" is a group of people who gather for a ritual.

Cunning folk – These professional and semi-professional magicians were active in Britain from about the Middle Ages to the turn of the century.

Dianic Wicca – A modern Pagan, goddess tradition that celebrates female empowerment and female experiences.

Divination – Trying to see the future or hidden things in the present.

Druids – The priestly elite of Ireland, Britain and modern-day France before Rome conquered Europe in the first century CE.

Evil eye – Commonly known as "the evils" or "stink eye" this ancient concept of a malevolent stare features in many cultures, leading to widespread superstitions.

Handfasting – Pledging something by shaking or joining hands.

Hex – An evil spell or a curse, but traditionally hex is also another word for witch.

Law of Attraction – This spiritual principle suggests that like attracts like and positive thinking can usher in a more positive reality.

Magick – Witches add the letter "k" to distinguish their practice from stage magic.

Manifestation – The act of materializing your wants and goals by genuinely believing in their possibility.

Pagan – Originally used as an insult to describe polytheists, later the term shifted to describe anyone who believed in "the false gods". Today, it's used as an umbrella term for occult and esoteric religions.

Runes – An ancient Nordic alphabet used for divination and magick.

Scrying – Another word for fortune-telling.

Sigil – Sigils are symbols that witches use in magick.

Vibration – The invisible or spiritual energy given off by objects or people.

Voodoo – A polytheistic religion from Africa. The word is also used to describe dolls or puppets used in magick. There's a misconception that they're used for harm or ill intent, but that isn't always the case.

Have you enjoyed this book? If so, find us on Facebook at **Summersdale Publishers**, on Twitter at **@Summersdale** and on Instagram at **@summersdalebooks** and get in touch. We'd love to hear from you!

www.summersdale.com